Revelations

GLORIA THOMAS

Revelations

VISIONS OF THE
SECOND COMING FROM THE
OLD AND NEW TESTAMENTS

Paintings by Gloria Thomas
Calligraphy and Illuminations by
Mary Breeden

Text Compiled and Arranged by
Mary Kathryn Lowell
Borders for Paintings by James Steele Hinton III

VIKING
STUDIO
BOOKS

The authors wish to give special thanks to Thomas and Clara Dupree, without whose patronage and encouragement the paintings in this book would never have been realized.

The painting of *St. John on Patmos* (which appears on page 52) and the watercolor study of the *Archangel Gabriel at the Annunication* (which appears on page 2) belong to Greene A. Settle, Jr., who has graciously given his permission for them to appear in this book. The painting of the *Angel on Land and Sea*, which appears on page 30 and on the slipcase, belongs to Ann Holt, who has also graciously given her permission for it to appear in this book. The remainder of the paintings hang in the Southern Baptist Theological Seminary, and the authors are grateful to that institution as well as to Gwen McClure, who was instrumental in arranging for their donation.

Finally, thanks are due to Jeff Carr for his expert photography of the paintings.

VIKING STUDIO BOOKS
Published by the Penguin Group
Penguin Books USA Inc., 375 Hudson Street, New York, New York 10014, U.S.A.
Penguin Books Ltd, 27 Wrights Lane, London W8 5TZ, England
Penguin Books Australia Ltd, Ringwood, Victoria, Australia
Penguin Books Canada Ltd, 10 Alcorn Avenue,
Toronto, Ontario, Canada M4V 3B2
Penguin Books (N.Z.) Ltd, 182–190 Wairau Road,
Auckland 10, New Zealand

Penguin Books Ltd, Registered Offices:
Harmondsworth, Middlesex, England

First published in 1994 by Viking Penguin,
a division of Penguin Books USA Inc.

1 3 5 7 9 10 8 6 4 2

Copyright © Sursum Corda, Inc., 1994
All rights reserved

ISBN 0-670-85581-2

CIP data available

Printed in Japan
Set in Post Antiqua
Front and back matter designed by Kathryn Parise

Preface

Then said I, "Lo, I come; in the volume of the book it is written of me."

—Psalm 40:7

The Apocalypse, or Revelation of St. John the Divine, has for nearly two millennia signified both promised redemption and impending calamity. Written during St. John's exile on the Isle of Patmos in the first century, it is a vision of Christ's triumphant return at the Consummation of the Ages. Appropriately, it is the final book of the Christian canon.

The text that follows is a hymn to the Second Coming of Our Lord. It was composed by drawing together scriptural images from the Apocalypse with fragments of prophecy from the Old Testament. Though the text is presented in seamless unity, the reader should be aware that it is a mingling of verses—a panorama of the visionary, the mystical, and the poetic descriptions of Christ's Parousia found throughout the Bible. A scriptural key follows the text so that the reader may explore the arrangement of passages.

—Mary Kathryn Lowell
Georgetown, Kentucky

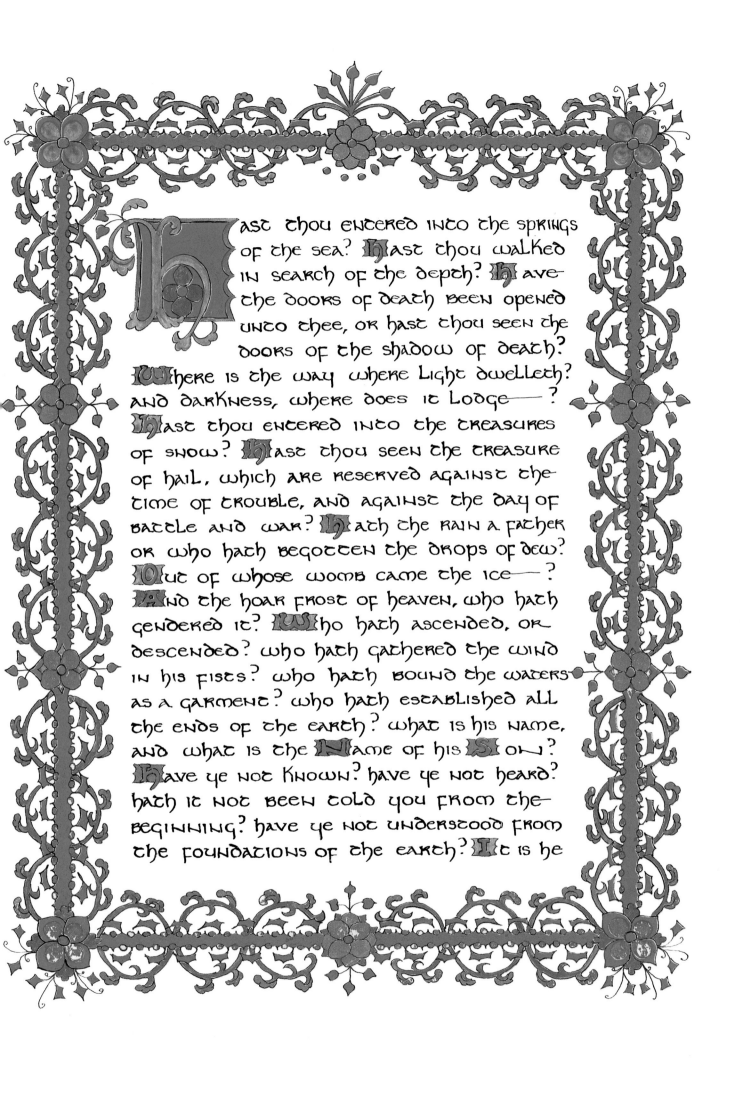

Hast thou entered into the springs of the sea? Hast thou walked in search of the depth? Have the doors of death been opened unto thee, or hast thou seen the doors of the shadow of death? Where is the way where Light dwelleth? and darkness, where does it lodge——? Hast thou entered into the treasures of snow? Hast thou seen the treasure of hail, which are reserved against the time of trouble, and against the day of battle and war? Hath the rain a father or who hath begotten the drops of dew? Out of whose womb came the ice——? And the hoar frost of heaven, who hath gendered it? Who hath ascended, or descended? who hath gathered the wind in his fists? who hath bound the waters as a garment? who hath established all the ends of the earth? what is his name, and what is the Name of his Son? Have ye not known? have ye not heard? hath it not been told you from the beginning? have ye not understood from the foundations of the earth? It is he

that sitteth upon the circle of the earth and the inhabitants thereof are as grass hoppers, that stretcheth out the heavens as a curtain and spreadeth them out as a tent to dwell in. I am the Lord, that is my name, and my glory will not give to another, neither my praise to graven images. I have made the earth and created man upon it, I even my hands have stretched out the heavens and all their host have I commanded. Who hath wrought and done it, calling the generations from the beginning? I the Lord, the first and the last, I am he. Be silent, O all flesh, before the Lord, for he is raised up out of his holy habi tation. The great day of the Lord is near and hasteth greatly, even the voice of the day of the Lord. I have a long time holden my peace, I have been still and refrained myself, now will I cry like a travailing woman, I will destroy and devour at once and I will punish the world for their iniquity, and I will cause the arrogancy of the proud to cease, and will lay low the haughtiness of the terrible. Judgement also will I lay to the line, and righteousness to the plummet: and the hail shall sweep away the refuge of lies, and the waters shall overflow the hiding place. Let the heavens be glad, and let the earth rejoice: and let men say among the nations, the Lord reigneth. Let the sea roar and the fullness thereof: Let the fields rejoice and all that is therein. Then shall the trees of the wood sing out at the presence of the Lord, because he cometh to judge the earth. For thus saith the Lord ✝ that created the heavens, God himself that formed the earth and made it, he created it not in vain, he formed it ✸ to be inhabited: I am the Lord and there is none else. I have not spoken in secret, in a dark place of the earth, I said not unto the seed of Jacob, Seek ye me in vain. Look unto me and be ye saved, all the ends of the earth: for I am God and there is none else. I have sworn by myself, the word is gone out of my mouth in righteousness and shall not return, that unto me every knee shall bow and every tongue shall swear.

And behold a throne set in heaven And He that sat upon the throne was to look upon like jasper and a sardine stone and there was a rainbow round about the throne. And in the midst of the throne were four living creatures. The first was like a lion, the second was like a calf and the third had a face as a man and the fourth was like a flying eagle. They had six wings each and they were full of eyes. And they rest not day or night saying Holy Holy Holy Lord God Almighty who was and is and who is to come.

And in the right hand of him that sat upon the throne was a book written within and on the backside, sealed with seven seals. And a strong angel proclaimed with a loud voice, Who is worthy, to open the book, to loosen the seals thereon? And no man in heaven, nor earth, neither under the earth was able to open the book neither to look thereon. And Lo, in the midst of the throne stood a Lamb as if it had been slain. His visage was so marred more than any other man, and his form more than the sons of men, and so hath he sprinkled many nations. Behold the Lamb of God. The Lion of the tribe of Judah, the Root of David hath prevailed to open the book, to loosen the seals. And he came and took the book out of the right hand of him that sat upon the throne. Listen, O isles, unto me, and hearken, ye people from far. the Lord hath called me from the womb, from the inward parts of my mother hath he made mention of my name. And he hath made my mouth like a sharp sword, in the shadow of his hand hath he hid me, and made me a polished shaft, in his quiver hath he hid me——.

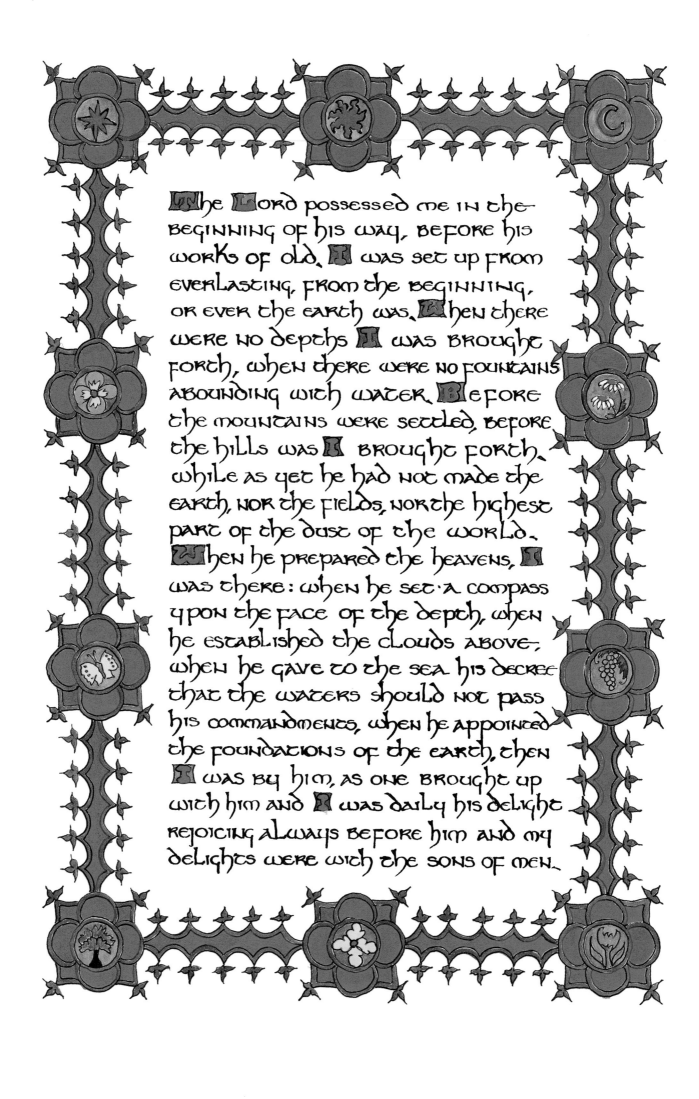

The Lord possessed me in the beginning of his way, before his works of old. I was set up from everlasting, from the beginning, or ever the earth was. When there were no depths I was brought forth, when there were no fountains abounding with water. Before the mountains were settled, before the hills was I brought forth. While as yet he had not made the earth, nor the fields, nor the highest part of the dust of the world. When he prepared the heavens, I was there: when he set a compass upon the face of the depth, when he established the clouds above, when he gave to the sea his decree that the waters should not pass his commandments, when he appointed the foundations of the earth, then I was by him, as one brought up with him and I was daily his delight rejoicing always before him and my delights were with the sons of men.

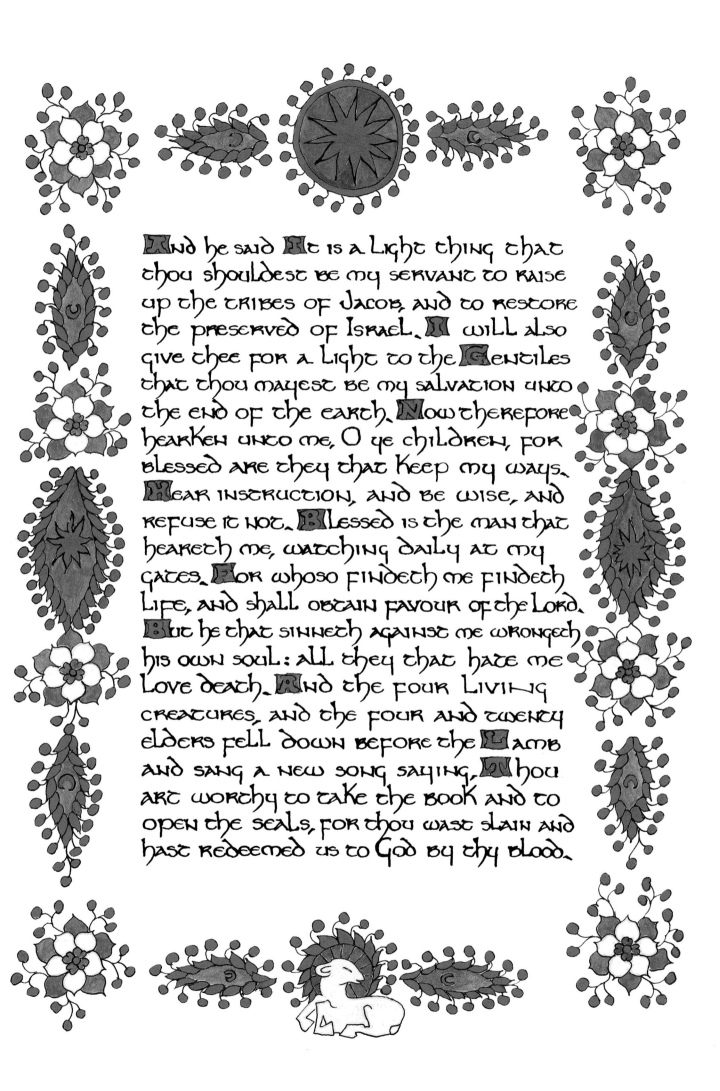

And he said It is a Light thing that thou shouldest be my servant to raise up the tribes of Jacob, and to restore the preserved of Israel. I will also give thee for a light to the Gentiles that thou mayest be my salvation unto the end of the earth. Now therefore hearken unto me, O ye children, for blessed are they that keep my ways. Hear instruction, and be wise, and refuse it not. Blessed is the man that heareth me, watching daily at my gates. For whoso findeth me findeth life, and shall obtain favour of the Lord. But he that sinneth against me wrongeth his own soul: all they that hate me love death. And the four living creatures, and the four and twenty elders fell down before the Lamb and sang a new song saying, Thou art worthy to take the book and to open the seals, for thou wast slain and hast redeemed us to God by thy blood.

And when the Lamb had opened one of the seven seals, one of the four living creatures said Come.

And behold, a white horse, and he that sat on him had a bow, and a crown was given him, and he went forth conquering, and to conquer. Know ye not this of old, that the triumphing of the wicked is short, and the joy of the hypocrite but for a moment. Flee from the iron weapon. Though he flee, the bow of bronze shall strike him through. It is drawn forth and comes out of the body. Yea terrors are upon him, and the glittering sword comes out of his gall.

ND when the
Lamb had
opened the
second seal, the
second creature
said, Come.

And there went out another horse
that was red and power was given
him that sat thereon to take peace
from the earth that men should kill
one another, and unto him was
given a great sword. For the Land
is full of bloody crimes, and the
city is full of violence. Destruction
cometh and men seek peace, and
there shall be none. A sword, a
sword is sharpened and furbished
to make a sore slaughter. It is
furbished that it may glitter and it
is given into the hand of the slayer.

And when the Lamb had opened the third seal, the third creature said, Come And Lo, a black horse, and he that sat on him had a pair of balances in his hand. And a voice in the midst of the creatures said, A measure of wheat for a penny and for a penny three measures of barley, and see that thou hurt not the wine nor the oil. The time is come, the day draweth near. Let not the buyer rejoice, nor the seller mourn for wrath is upon all the multitude. Cast the silver in the streets and the gold shall be removed. Silver and gold is not able to deliver in the day of the wrath of the Lord. They shall not satisfy the soul, nor fill the belly.

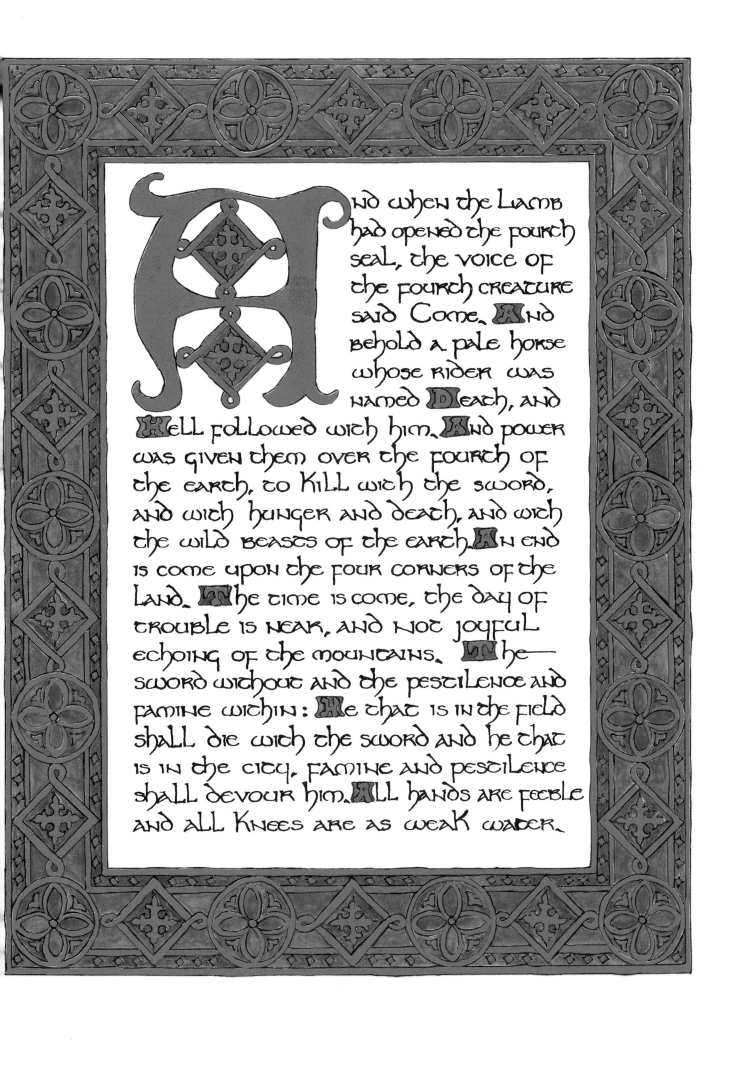

And when the Lamb had opened the fourth seal, the voice of the fourth creature said Come. And behold a pale horse whose rider was named Death, and Hell followed with him. And power was given them over the fourth of the earth, to kill with the sword, and with hunger and death, and with the wild beasts of the earth. An end is come upon the four corners of the land. The time is come, the day of trouble is near, and not joyful echoing of the mountains. The sword without and the pestilence and famine within: He that is in the field shall die with the sword and he that is in the city, famine and pestilence shall devour him. All hands are feeble and all knees are as weak water.

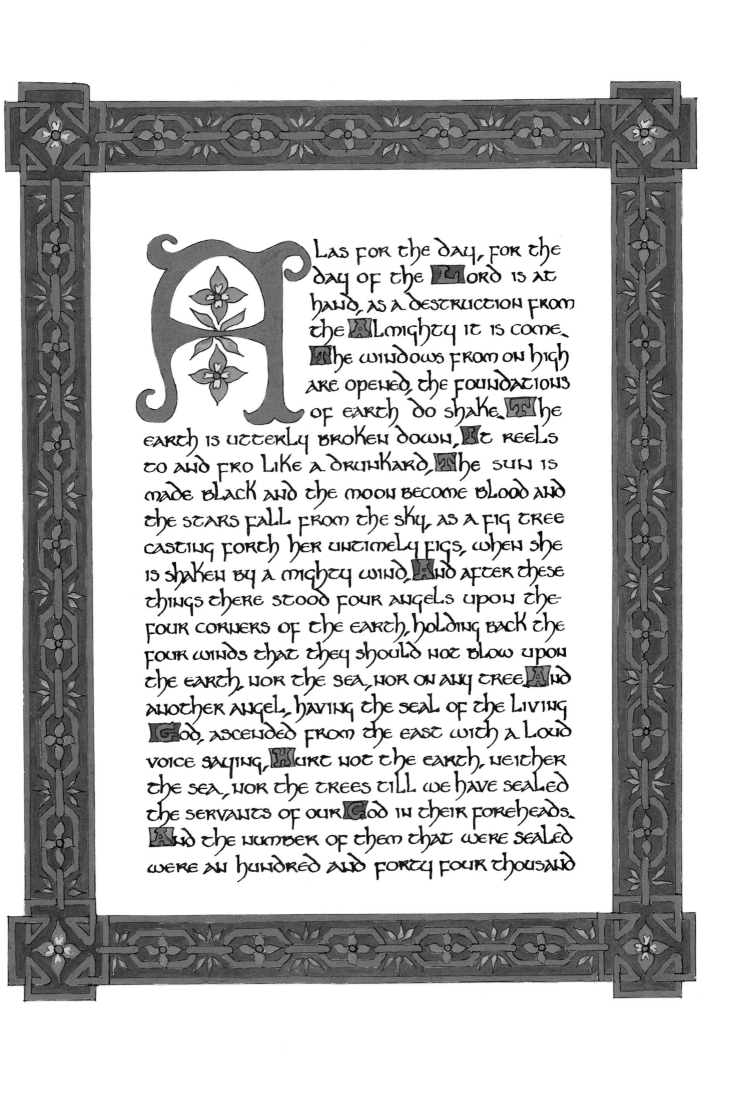

Alas for the day, for the day of the Lord is at hand, as a destruction from the Almighty it is come. The windows from on high are opened, the foundations of earth do shake. The earth is utterly broken down, it reels to and fro like a drunkard. The sun is made black and the moon become blood and the stars fall from the sky, as a fig tree casting forth her untimely figs, when she is shaken by a mighty wind. And after these things there stood four angels upon the four corners of the earth, holding back the four winds that they should not blow upon the earth, nor the sea, nor on any tree. And another angel, having the seal of the living God, ascended from the east with a loud voice saying, Hurt not the earth, neither the sea, nor the trees till we have sealed the servants of our God in their foreheads. And the number of them that were sealed were an hundred and forty four thousand

of all the tribes of the children of Israel.
Hear the word of the Lord, O ye nations,
and declare it in the isles afar off and say,
He that scattered Israel will gather him
and keep him, as a shepherd doth his flock.
But Zion said The Lord hath forsaken me
and my Lord hath forgotten me Can a woman
forget her sucking child, that she should not
have compassion in the son of her womb? yea
they may forget yet I will not forget thee.
Behold, I have graven thee upon the palms of
my hands, thy walls are continually before
me Thus saith the Lord, thy redeemer, and
he that formed thee from the womb Behold
I lift up my hand to the Gentiles, and set
up my standard to the people, and they shall
bring thy sons in their arms, and thy daughters
shall be carried upon their shoulders, And
an highway shall be there, and a way, and
it shall be called The way of holiness, the
unclean shall not pass over it, but the
redeemed shall walk there, and the ransomed
of the Lord shall return and come to Zion
with songs and everlasting joy upon their
heads, they shall obtain joy and gladness,
and sorrow and sighing shall flee away.

Let God arise, let his enemies be scattered, Let them also that hate him flee before him. As smoke is driven away, so drive them away, as wax melteth before the fire, so let the wicked perish at the presence of God. But let the righteous be glad, let them rejoice before God, yea let them exceedingly rejoice. Sing O heavens, and be joyful, O earth, and break forth into singing, O mountains, for the Lord hath comforted his people, and will have mercy upon his afflicted. For the Lord thy God in the midst of thee is mighty, he will save and rejoice over thee with joy, he will rest in his love and joy over thee with singing. And lo, a great multitude which no man could number, of all nations and kindreds and peoples and tongues, stood before the throne and before the Lamb, clothed with white robes and palms in their hands, saying, Salvation to our God, which sitteth upon the throne, and unto the Lamb. These are they which came out of great tribulation and have washed their robes and made them white in the blood of the Lamb. They shall hunger no more, for the Lamb shall feed them, and lead them unto living fountains and God shall wipe away all tears from their eyes.

And seven angels stood before God, and unto them were given seven trumpets, and they prepared themselves to sound. Hear, all ye people and hearken, O earth, all that therein is, for behold the Lord cometh forth out of his holy place and he will come down and tread upon the high places. The mountains shall be molten under his feet, and the valleys cleft as wax before the fire. So that the fishes of the sea, and the fowls of the heaven, and the beasts of the field, and all that creepeth upon the earth and all the men shall shake at his presence. And the first angel sounded and there followed hail and fire mingled with blood, and they were cast upon the earth, and a third of the trees and all the green grass was burned. And the second angel sounded, and as it were a great mountain burning with fire was cast into the sea, and a third part of the sea became blood, and a third of the creatures died and a third of the ships were destroyed.

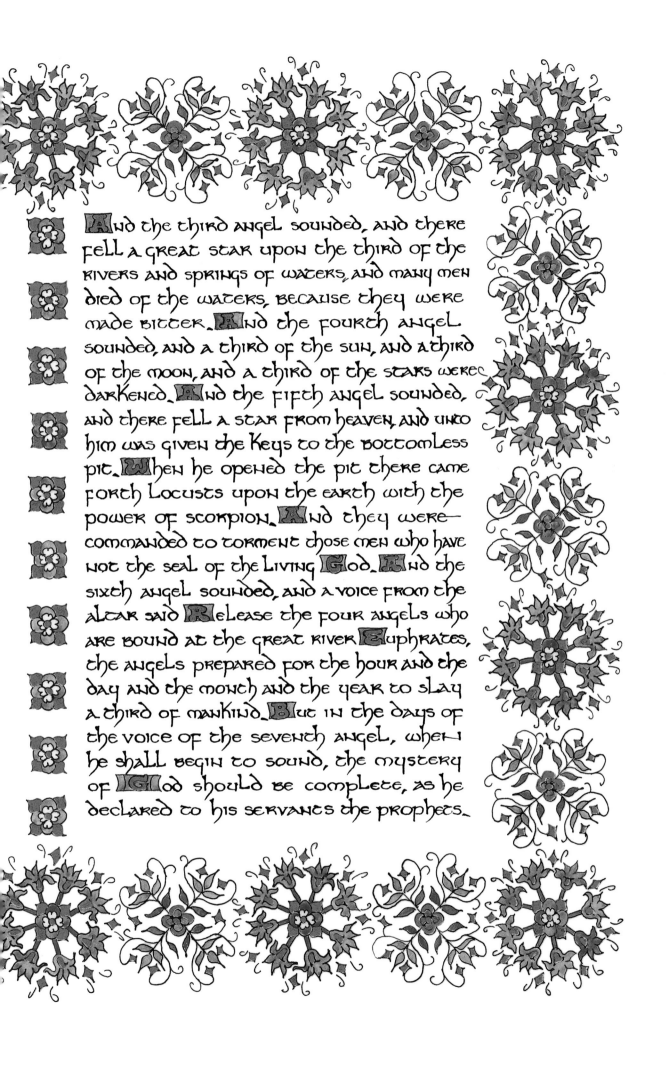

And the third angel sounded, and there fell a great star upon the third of the rivers and springs of waters, and many men died of the waters, because they were made bitter. And the fourth angel sounded, and a third of the sun, and a third of the moon, and a third of the stars were darkened. And the fifth angel sounded, and there fell a star from heaven, and unto him was given the keys to the bottomless pit. When he opened the pit there came forth locusts upon the earth with the power of scorpion. And they were commanded to torment those men who have not the seal of the living God. And the sixth angel sounded, and a voice from the altar said Release the four angels who are bound at the great river Euphrates, the angels prepared for the hour and the day and the month and the year to slay a third of mankind. But in the days of the voice of the seventh angel, when he shall begin to sound, the mystery of God should be complete, as he declared to his servants the prophets.

The Lord hath prepared his throne in the heavens, and his kingdom ruleth over all. Hell is naked before him, and destruction hath no covering. He stretcheth out the north over the empty place, and hangeth the earth upon nothing. He hath compassed the waters with bounds until the day and night come to an end. The pillars of heaven tremble and are astonished at his reproof. As for man, his days are as grass, as a flower of the field so he flourisheth. For the wind passeth over it and it is gone, and the place thereof shall know it no more. But the mercy of the Lord is from everlasting to everlasting upon them that fear him, and his righteousness unto children's children. And another mighty angel came down from heaven, and he set his right foot upon the sea, and his left foot on the earth, and lifted up his hand to heaven, and sware by him that liveth for ever and ever that there should be time no longer.

And behold I will give power unto my two witnesses, and they will prophesy a thousand two hundred and three score days, clothed in sackcloth. And these are the two olive trees and the two candlesticks standing before the God of the earth. And when they shall have finished their testimony, the beast that ascendeth out of the bottomless pit shall make war with them, and overcome and kill them. And after three days and an half the Spirit of Life from God entered them, and they stood upon their feet. And they ascended up into heaven in a cloud, and their enemies beheld them.

And the seventh angel sounded, and there were great voices in heaven saying The Kingdoms of this world are become the Kingdoms of our Lord and of his Christ and he shall reign for ever and ever. We give thee thanks O Lord God Almighty who is, and was, and who is to come, because thou hast taken to thee thy great power, and hast reigned. And the nations were angry, and thy wrath is come, and the time of the dead that they should be judged, and that thou shouldest give reward unto thy servants the prophets, and to the saints, and to them that fear thee both great and small, and shouldest destroy them which destroy the earth.

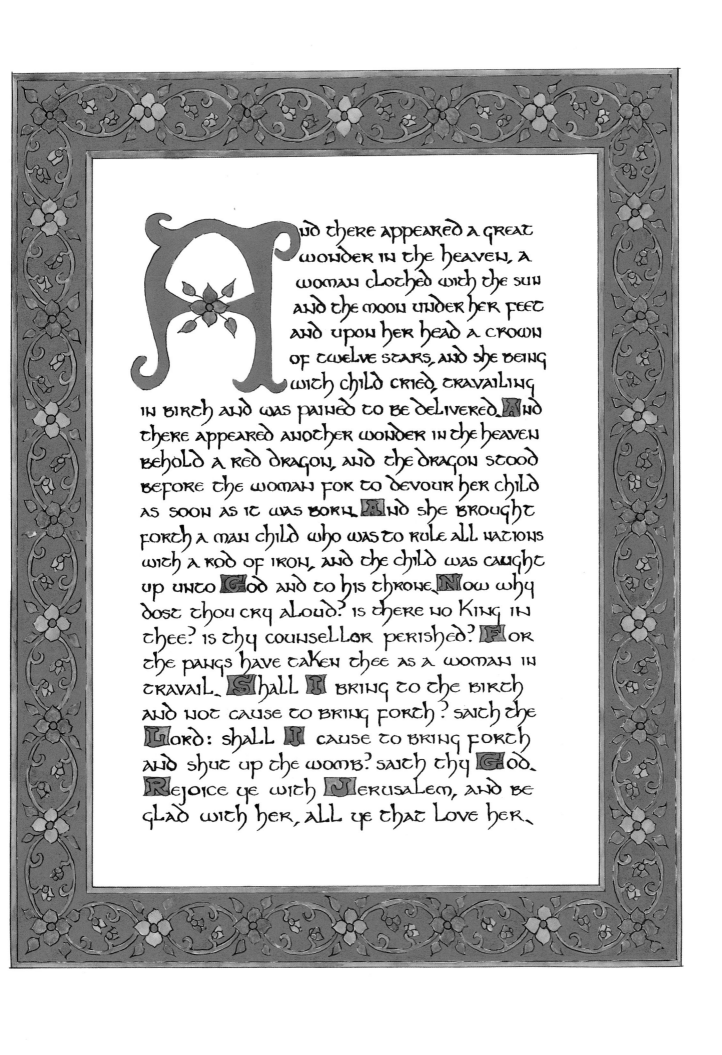

And there appeared a great wonder in the heaven, a woman clothed with the sun and the moon under her feet and upon her head a crown of twelve stars, and she being with child cried, travailing in birth and was pained to be delivered. And there appeared another wonder in the heaven behold a red dragon, and the dragon stood before the woman for to devour her child as soon as it was born. And she brought forth a man child who was to rule all nations with a rod of iron, and the child was caught up unto God and to his throne. Now why dost thou cry aloud? is there no king in thee? is thy counsellor perished? For the pangs have taken thee as a woman in travail. Shall I bring to the birth and not cause to bring forth? saith the Lord: shall I cause to bring forth and shut up the womb? saith thy God. Rejoice ye with Jerusalem, and be glad with her, all ye that love her.

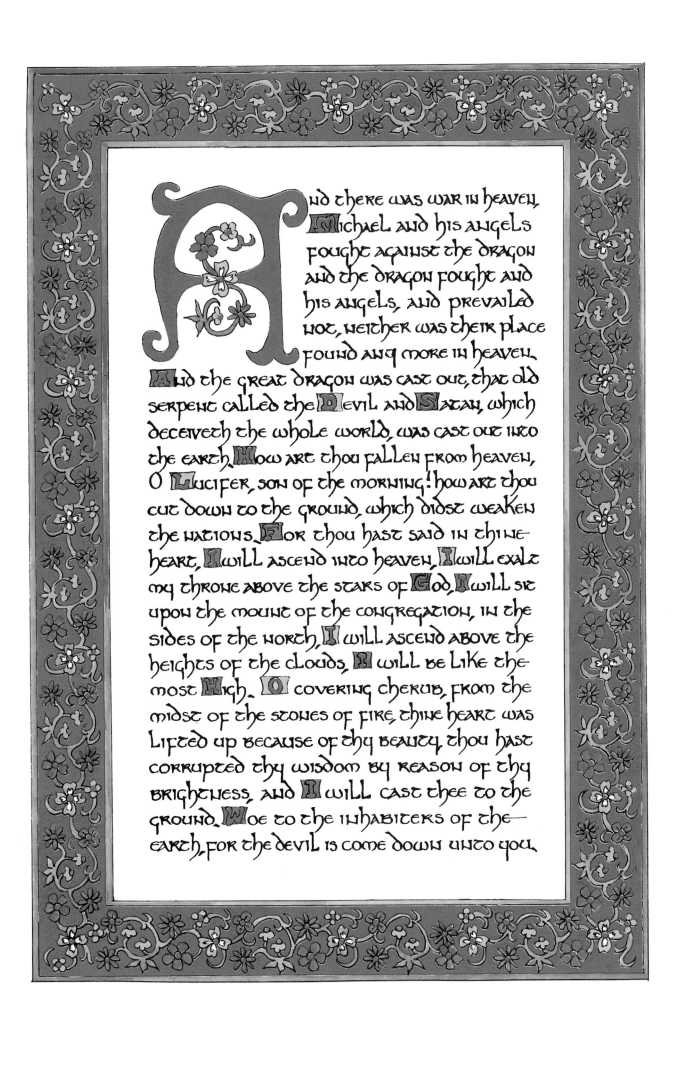

And there was war in heaven, Michael and his angels fought against the dragon and the dragon fought and his angels, and prevailed not, neither was their place found any more in heaven. And the great dragon was cast out, that old serpent called the Devil and Satan, which deceiveth the whole world: was cast out into the earth. How art thou fallen from heaven, O Lucifer, son of the morning! how art thou cut down to the ground, which didst weaken the nations. For thou hast said in thine heart, I will ascend into heaven, I will exalt my throne above the stars of God, I will sit upon the mount of the congregation, in the sides of the north, I will ascend above the heights of the clouds, I will be like the most High. O covering cherub, from the midst of the stones of fire, thine heart was lifted up because of thy beauty, thou hast corrupted thy wisdom by reason of thy brightness, and I will cast thee to the ground. Woe to the inhabiters of the earth, for the devil is come down unto you,

And an angel did fly in the midst of heaven, having the everlasting gospel, saying with a loud voice, Fear God, and give glory to him, for the hour of his judgement is come, and worship him that made heaven, and earth, and the sea, and the fountains of waters. And there appeared another sign in heaven, great and marvelous, seven angels having the seven last plagues. The temple in heaven was opened and the seven angels came out of the temple. And them that had gotten the victory did sing the song of Moses, and the song of the Lamb, saying, Great and marvelous are thy works, Lord God Almighty, just and true are thy ways, thou King of saints. Who shall not fear thee and glorify thy name, for thou only art holy, for all nations shall come and worship before thee, for thy judgements are made manifest. And a great voice out of the temple said, Go your ways and pour out the vials of the wrath of God upon the earth.

ND the water of the great river Euphrates
was dried up, that the way of the kings of
the east might be prepared. And the kings of
the whole world were gathered together to the battle
of that great day of the Almighty. And they were

gathered into a place called Armageddon. Proclaim ye this among the Gentiles, Prepare war, wake up the mighty men, Let all the men of war draw near. Beat your plowshares into swords, and your scythes into spears. Let the weak say I am strong. Assemble yourselves and come, all ye heathen, and gather yourselves together round about, thither cause thy mighty ones to come down, O Lord. Let the heathen be wakened, and come up to the valley, for there will I sit to judge all the heathen round about. Put ye in the sickle, for the harvest is ripe, come, get you down, for the press is full, the fats overflow for their wickedness is great. Multitudes, multitudes in the valley of decision, for the day of the Lord is near in the valley of decision. The Lord shall roar out of Zion, and utter his voice in Jerusalem, and the heavens and the earth shall shake. In the hand of the Lord there is a cup, and he poureth out the wine that is red and full. Surely the wicked of the earth must drain the cup and drink it down to the dregs. And there came a great voice out of heaven saying, It is done, It is done.

Come hither, and see the judgment of the great harlot that sitteth upon many waters, with whom the kings of the earth have committed fornication, and the inhabitants of the earth have been made drunk with the wine of her fornication. Come hither and see a woman arrayed in scarlet and purple, having a golden cup in her hand, full of abominations and filth of fornication. Come hither and see, she sits upon a scarlet coloured beast full of names of blasphemy, having seven heads and ten horns, a woman drunken with the blood of the martyrs of Jesus. And upon her forehead was written a name of mystery, Babylon the Great, the Mother of Harlots and Abominations of the Earth. Come down and sit in the dust, O virgin daughter of Babylon, sit on the ground with no throne. For thou, O daughter of Chaldeans, art no more tender and delicate. Uncover thy locks, make bare the leg, uncover the thigh, pass over the rivers. Show the nations thy nakedness, and the kingdoms thy shame. Stand with thine enchantments, thy multitude of sorceries. Let now the astrologers and stargazers save thee from the things which shall come upon thee. Alas, great city, what city is like this great city, wherein were made rich all they that had ships in the sea? Merchants of the earth, weep and mourn over her. Come out of her, oh my people, that ye be not partakers of her sins. Rejoice over her, thou heaven, rejoice ye holy apostles and prophets rejoice. Babylon is fallen, is fallen, thrown down with violence and become the habitation of dragons.

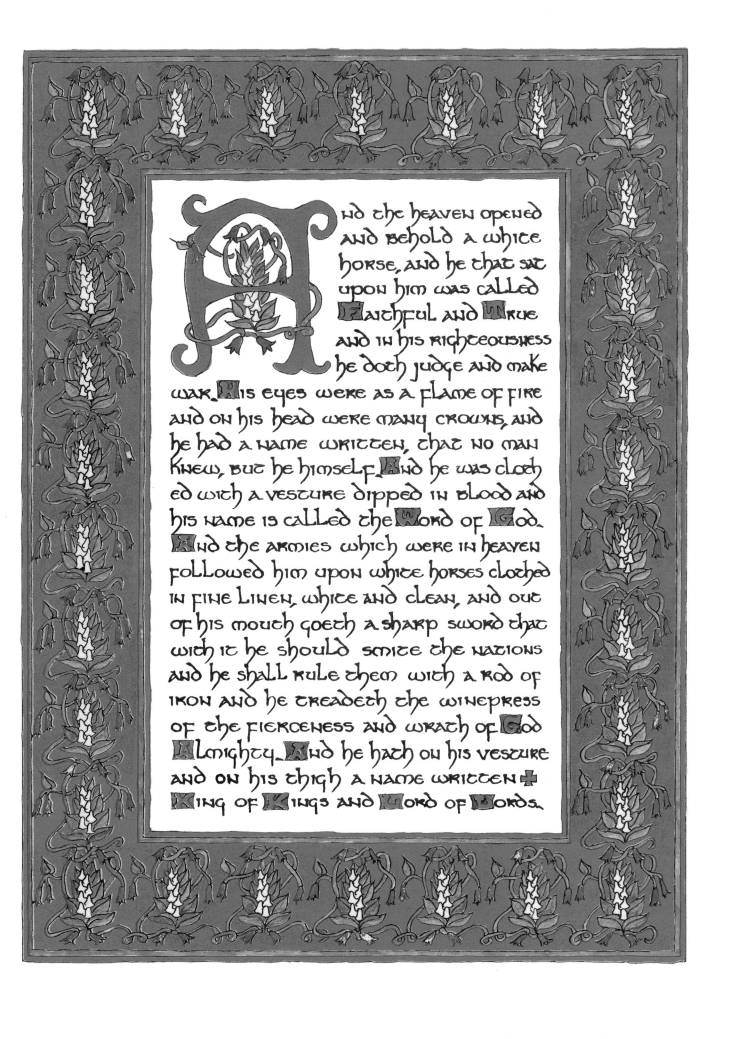

And the heaven opened and behold a white horse, and he that sat upon him was called Faithful and True and in his righteousness he doth judge and make war. His eyes were as a flame of fire and on his head were many crowns, and he had a name written, that no man knew, but he himself. And he was clothed with a vesture dipped in blood and his name is called the Word of God. And the armies which were in heaven followed him upon white horses clothed in fine linen, white and clean, and out of his mouth goeth a sharp sword that with it he should smite the nations and he shall rule them with a rod of iron and he treadeth the winepress of the fierceness and wrath of God Almighty. And he hath on his vesture and on his thigh a name written ✠ King of Kings and Lord of Lords.

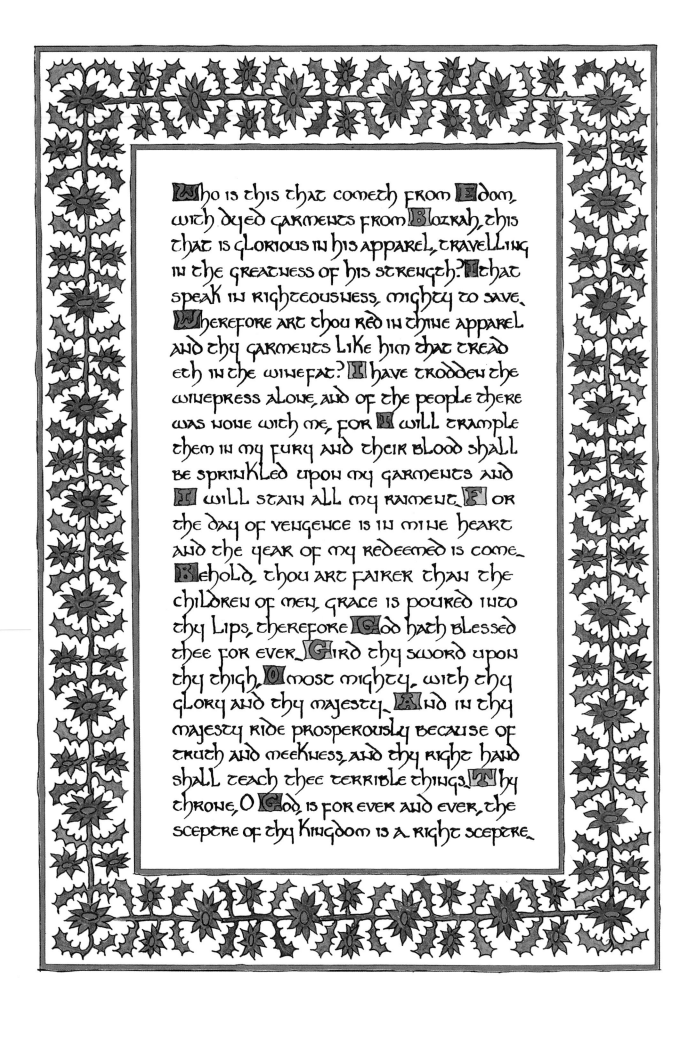

Who is this that cometh from Edom, with dyed garments from Bozrah, this that is glorious in his apparel, travelling in the greatness of his strength? I that speak in righteousness, mighty to save. Wherefore art thou red in thine apparel and thy garments like him that treadeth in the winefat? I have trodden the winepress alone, and of the people there was none with me, for I will trample them in my fury and their blood shall be sprinkled upon my garments and I will stain all my raiment. For the day of vengence is in mine heart and the year of my redeemed is come. Behold, thou art fairer than the children of men, grace is poured into thy lips, therefore God hath blessed thee for ever. Gird thy sword upon thy thigh, O most mighty, with thy glory and thy majesty. And in thy majesty ride prosperously because of truth and meekness, and thy right hand shall teach thee terrible things. Thy throne, O God, is for ever and ever, the sceptre of thy kingdom is a right sceptre.

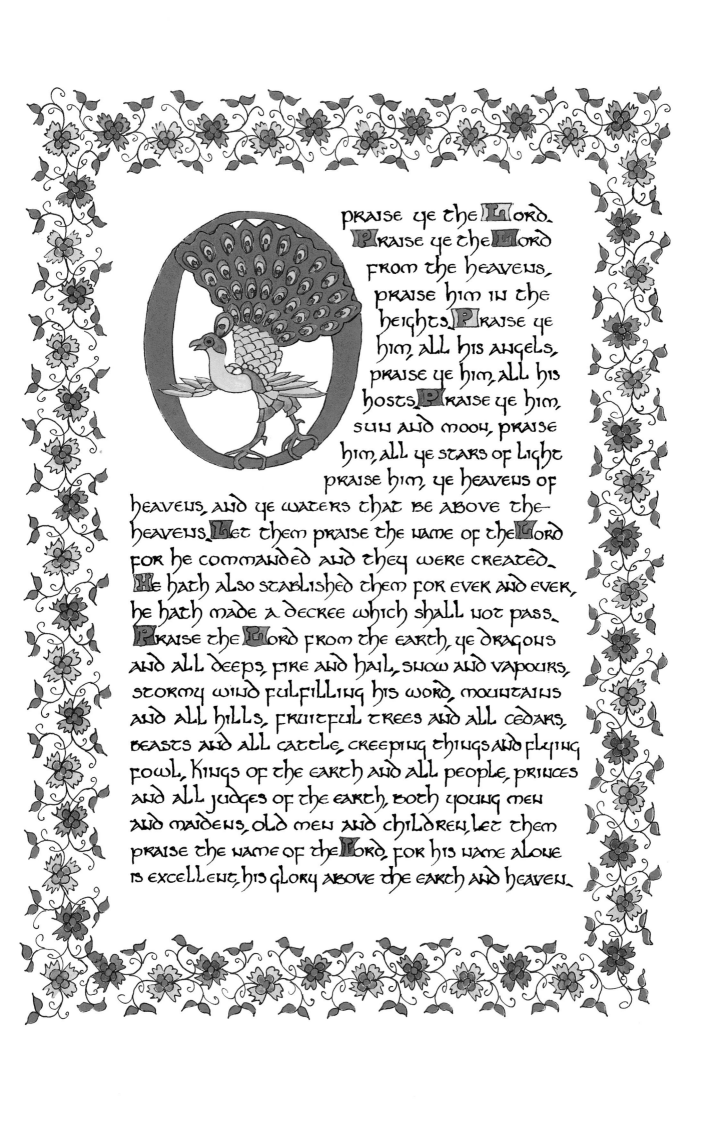

PRAISE YE THE LORD. PRAISE YE THE LORD FROM THE HEAVENS, PRAISE HIM IN THE HEIGHTS. PRAISE YE HIM, ALL HIS ANGELS, PRAISE YE HIM, ALL HIS HOSTS. PRAISE YE HIM, SUN AND MOON, PRAISE HIM, ALL YE STARS OF LIGHT PRAISE HIM, YE HEAVENS OF HEAVENS, AND YE WATERS THAT BE ABOVE THE HEAVENS. LET THEM PRAISE THE NAME OF THE LORD FOR HE COMMANDED AND THEY WERE CREATED. HE HATH ALSO STABLISHED THEM FOR EVER AND EVER, HE HATH MADE A DECREE WHICH SHALL NOT PASS. PRAISE THE LORD FROM THE EARTH, YE DRAGONS AND ALL DEEPS, FIRE AND HAIL, SNOW AND VAPOURS, STORMY WIND FULFILLING HIS WORD, MOUNTAINS AND ALL HILLS, FRUITFUL TREES AND ALL CEDARS, BEASTS AND ALL CATTLE, CREEPING THINGS AND FLYING FOWL, KINGS OF THE EARTH AND ALL PEOPLE, PRINCES AND ALL JUDGES OF THE EARTH, BOTH YOUNG MEN AND MAIDENS, OLD MEN AND CHILDREN, LET THEM PRAISE THE NAME OF THE LORD, FOR HIS NAME ALONE IS EXCELLENT, HIS GLORY ABOVE THE EARTH AND HEAVEN.

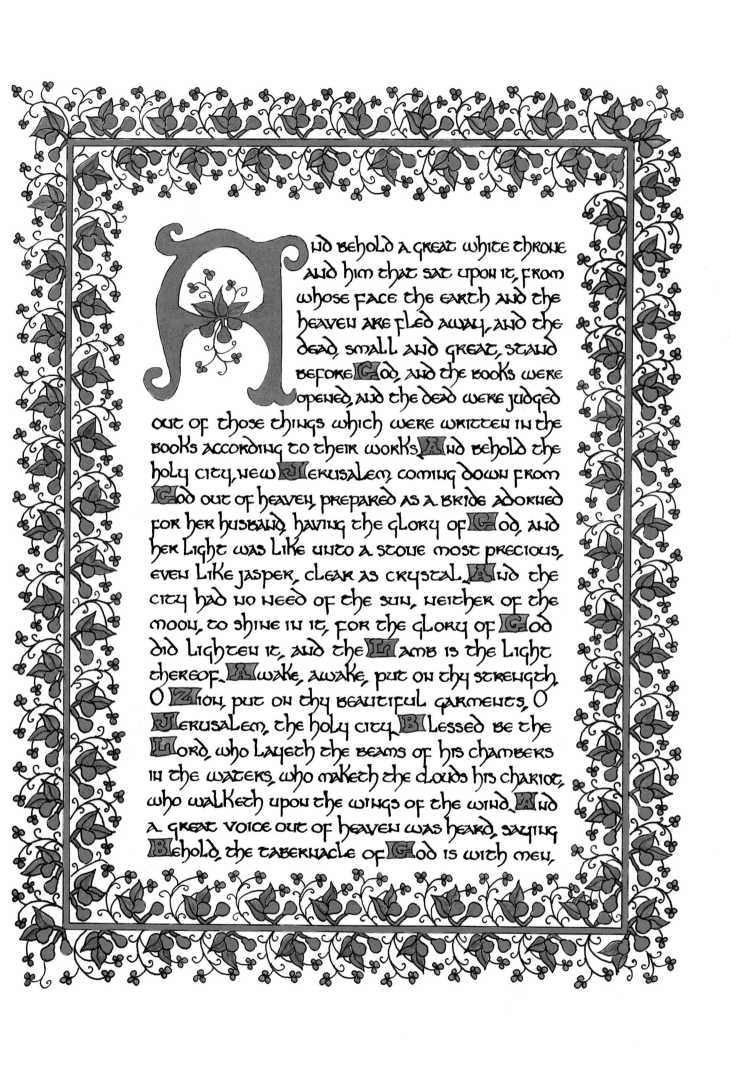

And behold a great white throne and him that sat upon it, from whose face the earth and the heaven are fled away, and the dead, small and great, stand before God, and the books were opened, and the dead were judged out of those things which were written in the books according to their works. And behold the holy city, new Jerusalem, coming down from God out of heaven, prepared as a bride adorned for her husband, having the glory of God, and her light was like unto a stone most precious, even like jasper, clear as crystal. And the city had no need of the sun, neither of the moon, to shine in it, for the glory of God did lighten it, and the Lamb is the light thereof. Awake, awake, put on thy strength, O Zion, put on thy beautiful garments, O Jerusalem, the holy city. Blessed be the Lord, who layeth the beams of his chambers in the waters, who maketh the clouds his chariot, who walketh upon the wings of the wind. And a great voice out of heaven was heard, saying Behold, the tabernacle of God is with men,

And he will dwell with them, and they shall be his people. And God shall wipe away all tears from their eyes, and there shall be no more death, neither sorrow, nor crying, neither shall there be any more pain, for the former things are passed away. And there shall be no more curse. O clap your hands, all ye people, shout unto God with a voice of triumph. Behold I make all things new. It is done. I am Alpha and Omega, the beginning and the end. I will give unto him that is athirst of the fountain of the water of life freely. I am he that liveth, and was dead, and behold I am alive forevermore, Amen, and have the keys of hell and death. Behold, I create new heavens and a new earth, and the former shall not be remembered, nor brought to mind. But be ye glad and rejoice forever in that which I create for behold, I create Jerusalem a rejoicing, and her people a joy. Praise ye the Lord. Praise God in his sanctuary, praise him in the firmament of his power. Praise him for his mighty acts, praise him according to his excellent greatness. Let everything that hath breath praise the Lord. Praise ye the Lord. Even so, come Lord Jesus. The grace of our Lord Jesus Christ be with you all. Amen and Amen.

THE TEXT
AND SCRIPTURAL KEY

In 1971, my friend Gloria Thomas approached me with the idea of creating a book of meditations on the Second Coming of Christ. She was planning a series of paintings based on the Apocalyptic vision of St. John and needed a scriptural key to accompany it. In response, I developed a text around Gloria's images by selecting and arranging Biblical passages that are prophetically associated with the Apocalypse. A scriptural key to this arrangement is provided on the following pages.

While the chronological appearance of images in the book closely follows St. John's vision, I have surrounded each with a chorus of passages gathered from various places in the Bible to form, as it were, a single hymn. In much the same way, the liturgical poets Sts. Basil the Great and John Chrysostom composed the order of Christian worship by uniting Old Testament passages, which anticipate Christ's Messianic career, with New Testament references, which detail its fulfillment.

My choice of passages was guided by Holy Tradition and the cross-references in Bible concordances. What is unique to this text is the way in which these verses, though drawn from many prophetic voices in the Bible, are freely interwoven and subtly placed end to end to effect the unbroken cadence of an epic poem. For the most part, the original syntax of verses has been preserved, but I have used "poetic license" to enhance the rhythmical quality of the text and to facilitate a smooth transition between verses.

Though the meaning of the Bible's wording has not been altered, I took the liberty of changing some verb tenses for consistent agreement. In certain passages I also made minor word changes and introduced a stylistic repetition of phrases to carry the poetic momentum. This book should not be mistaken for an exact transcription of the Bible; it is, rather, a thematic arrangement of sacred text similar to that found in an oratorio. The key will guide the interested reader in charting the lyrical fusion of passages appearing in the text, which is offered simply as a song to "The Last Things" and not as an authoritative source for study or doctrine.

—MARY KATHRYN LOWELL

Hast thou entered into the springs of the sea? Hast thou walked in search of the depth? Have the doors of death been opened unto thee, or hast thou seen the doors of the shadow of death? Where is the way where light dwelleth? and darkness, where does it lodge? Hast thou entered into the treasures of snow? Hast thou seen the treasure of hail, which are reserved against the time of trouble, and against the day of battle and war? Hath the rain a father or who hath begotten the drops of dew? Out of whose womb came the ice—? And the hoar frost of heaven, who hath gendered it? (Job 38:16-17, 19, 22-23, 28-29) Who hath ascended, or descended? Who hath gathered the wind in his fists? Who hath bound the waters as a garment? Who hath established all the ends of the earth? What is his name, and what is the Name of his Son? (Proverbs 30:4) Have ye not known? have ye not heard? hath it not been told you from the beginning? have ye not understood from the foundations of the earth? It is he that sitteth upon the circle of the earth and the inhabitants thereof are as grasshoppers, that stretcheth out the heavens as a curtain and spreadeth them out as a tent to dwell in. (Isaiah 40:21, 22) I am the Lord: that is my name, and my glory will I not give to another, neither my praise to graven images. (Isaiah 42:8) I have made the earth and created man upon it: I even my hands have stretched out the heavens and all their host have I commanded. (Isaiah 45:12) Who hath wrought and done it, calling the generations from the beginning? I the Lord, the first and the last, I am he. (Isaiah 41:4) Be silent, O all flesh, before the Lord, for he is raised up out of his holy habitation. (Zechariah 2:13) The great day of the Lord is near and hasteth greatly, even the voice of the day of the Lord. (Zephaniah 1:14) I have a long time holden my peace, I have been still and refrained myself: now will I cry like a travailing woman, I will destroy and devour at once (Isaiah 42:14) and I will punish the world for their iniquity, and I will cause the arrogancy of the proud to cease, and will lay low the haughtiness of the terrible, (Isaiah 13:11) judgement also will I lay to the line, and righteousness to the plummet: and the hail shall sweep away the refuge of lies, and the waters shall overflow the hiding place. (Isaiah 28:17) Let the heavens be glad, and let the earth rejoice: and let men say among the nations, the Lord reigneth. Let the sea roar and the fullness thereof: let the fields rejoice and all that is therein. Then shall the trees of the wood sing out at the presence of the Lord, because he cometh to judge the earth. (I Chronicles 16:31-33) For thus saith the Lord that created the heavens, God himself that formed the earth and made it, he created it not in vain, he formed it to be inhabited: I am the Lord and there is none else. I have not spoken in secret, in a dark place of the earth, I said not unto the seed of Jacob, Seek ye me in vain. (Isaiah 45:18, 19) Look unto me and be ye saved, all the ends of the earth: for I am God and there is none else, I have sworn by myself, the word is gone out of my mouth in righteousness and shall not return, that unto me every knee shall bow and every tongue shall swear. (Isaiah 45:22-23)

And behold a throne set in heaven and He that sat upon the throne was to look upon like jasper and a sardine stone and there was a rainbow round about the throne. And in the midst of the throne were four living creatures. The first was like a lion, the second was like a calf and the third had a face as a man and the fourth was like a flying eagle. (Revelation 4:2, 3, 6, 7) They had six wings each and they were full of eyes. And they rest not day or night saying Holy Holy Holy Lord God Almighty who was and is and who is to come. (Revelation 4:8) And in the right hand of him that sat upon the throne was a book written within and on the backside, sealed with seven seals. And a strong angel proclaimed with a loud voice, Who is worthy, to open the book, to loosen the seals thereon? And no man in heaven, nor earth, neither under the earth was able to open the book neither to look thereon. (Revelation 5:1-3) And Lo, in the midst of the throne stood a Lamb as if it had been slain. (Revelation 5:6) His visage was so marred more than any other man, and his form more than the sons of men, and so hath he sprinkled many nations. (Isaiah 52:14, 15) Behold the Lamb of God. (John 1:36) The Lion of the tribe of Judah, the Root of David hath prevailed to open the book, to loosen the seals. (Revelation 5:5) And he came and took the book out of the right hand of him that sat upon the throne. (Revelation 5:7) Listen, O isles, unto me, and hearken, ye people from far, the Lord hath called me from the womb, from the inward parts of my mother hath he made mention of my name. And he hath made my mouth like a sharp sword, in the shadow of his hand hath he hid me, and made me a polished shaft, in his quiver hath he hid me. (Isaiah 49:1, 2) The Lord possessed me in the beginning of his way, before his works of old. I was set up from everlasting, from the beginning, or ever the earth was. When there were no depths I was brought forth, when there were no fountains abounding with water. Before the mountains were settled, before the hills was I brought forth, while as yet he had not made the earth, nor the fields, nor the highest part of the dust of the world. When he prepared the heavens, I was there: when he set a compass upon the face of the depth, when he established the clouds above, when he gave to the sea his decree that the waters should not pass his commandments, when he appointed the foundations of the earth, then I was by him, as one brought up with him and I was daily his delight rejoicing always before him and my delights were with the sons of men. (Proverbs 8:22-31) And he said, It is a light thing that thou shouldest be my servant to raise up the tribes of Jacob, and to restore the preserved of Israel. I will also give thee for a light to the Gentiles that thou mayest be my salvation unto the end of the earth. (Isaiah 49:6) Now therefore hearken unto me, O ye children, for blessed are they that keep my ways. Hear instruction, and be wise, and refuse it not. Blessed is the man that heareth me, watching daily at my gates. For whoso findeth me, findeth life, and shall obtain favour of the Lord. But he that sinneth against me wrongeth his own soul: all they that hate me love death. (Proverbs 8:32-36) And the four living creatures, and the four and twenty elders fell down before the Lamb and sang a new song saying, Thou art worthy to take the book and to open the seals, for thou wast slain and hast redeemed us to God by thy blood. (Revelation 5:8, 9)

And when the Lamb had opened one of the seven seals, one of the four living creatures said, Come. And behold, a white horse, and he that sat on him had a bow, and a crown was given him, and he went forth conquering, and to conquer. (Revelation 6:1, 2) Know ye not this of old, that the triumphing of the wicked is short, and the joy of the hypocrite but for a moment. Flee from the iron weapon. Though he flee, the bow of bronze shall strike him through. It is drawn forth and comes out of the body. Yea, terrors are upon him, and the glittering sword comes out of his gall. (Job 20:4, 5, 24, 25)

And when the Lamb had opened the second seal, the second creature said, Come. And there went out another horse that was red and power was given him that sat thereon to take peace from the earth that men should kill one another, and unto him was given a great sword. (Revelation 6:3, 4) For the land is full of bloody crimes, and the city is full of violence. Destruction cometh and men seek peace, and there shall be none. (Ezekiel 7:23, 25) A sword, a sword is sharpened and furbished to make a sore slaughter. It is furbished that it may glitter and it is given into the hand of the slayer. (Ezekiel 21:9-10, 11)

And when the Lamb had opened the third seal, the third creature said, Come. And lo, a black horse, and he that sat on him had a pair of balances in his hand. And a voice in the midst of the creatures said, A measure of wheat for a penny and for a penny three measures of barley, and see that thou hurt not the wine nor the oil. (Revelation 6:5, 6) The time is come, the day draweth near. Let not the buyer rejoice, nor the seller mourn for wrath is upon all the multitude. Cast the silver in the streets and the gold shall be removed. Silver and gold is not able to deliver in the day of the wrath of the Lord. They shall not satisfy the soul, nor fill the belly. (Ezekiel 7:12, 19)

And when the Lamb had opened the fourth seal, the voice of the fourth creature said, Come. And behold a pale horse whose rider was named Death, and Hell followed with him. And power was given them over the fourth of the earth, to kill with the sword, and with hunger and death, and with the wild beasts of the earth. (Revelation 6:7, 8) An end is come upon the four corners of the land. The time is come, the day of trouble is near, and not joyful echoing of the mountains. The sword without and the pestilence and famine within: He that is in the field shall die with the sword and he that is in the city, famine and pestilence shall devour him. All hands are feeble and all knees are as weak water. (Ezekiel 7:2, 7, 15, 17)

FOUR WINDS   Pages 22-25

Alas for the day, for the day of the Lord is at hand, as a destruction from the Almighty it is come. (Joel 1:15) The windows from on high are opened, the foundations of earth do shake. The earth is utterly broken down, It reels to and fro like a drunkard. (Isaiah 24:18, 19, 20) The sun is made

black and the moon become blood and the stars fall from the sky, as a fig tree casting forth her untimely figs, when she is shaken by a mighty wind. (Revelation 6:12, 13) And after these things there stood four angels upon the four corners of the earth, holding back the four winds that they should not blow upon the earth, nor the sea, nor on any tree. And another angel, having the seal of the living God, ascended from the east with a loud voice saying, Hurt not the earth, neither the sea, nor the trees till we have sealed the servants of our God in their foreheads. And the number of them that were sealed were an hundred and forty four thousand of all the tribes of the children of Israel. (Revelation 7:1-4) Hear the word of the Lord, O ye nations, and declare it in the isles afar off and say, He that scattered Israel will gather him and keep him, as a shepherd doth his flock. (Jeremiah 31:10) But Zion said, The Lord hath forsaken me and my Lord hath forgotten me. Can a woman forget her sucking child, that she should not have compassion in the son of her womb? yea they may forget yet I will not forget thee. Behold, I have graven thee upon the palms of my hands, thy walls are continually before me. (Isaiah 49:14-16) Thus saith the Lord, thy redeemer, and he that formed thee from the womb. (Isaiah 44:24) Behold, I lift up my hand to the Gentiles, and set up my standard to the people, and they shall bring thy sons in their arms, and thy daughters shall be carried upon their shoulders. (Isaiah 49:22) And an highway shall be there, and a way, and it shall be called The way of holiness, the unclean shall not pass over it, (Isaiah 35:8) but the redeemed shall walk there, (Isaiah 35:9) and the ransomed of the Lord shall return and come to Zion with songs and everlasting joy upon their heads, they shall obtain joy and gladness, and sorrow and sighing shall flee away. (Isaiah 35:10) Let God arise, let his enemies be scattered, let them also that hate him flee before him. As smoke is driven away, so drive them away, as wax melteth before the fire, so let the wicked perish at the presence of God. But let the righteous be glad, let them rejoice before God, yea let them exceedingly rejoice. (Psalm 68:1-3) Sing O heavens, and be joyful, O earth, and break forth into singing, O mountains, for the Lord hath comforted his people, and will have mercy upon his afflicted. (Isaiah 49:13) For the Lord thy God in the midst of thee is mighty, he will save and rejoice over thee with joy, he will rest in his love and joy over thee with singing. (Zephaniah 3:17) And lo, a great multitude which no man could number, of all nations and kindreds and peoples and tongues, stood before the throne and before the Lamb, clothed with white robes and palms in their hands, saying, Salvation to our God, which sitteth upon the throne, and unto the Lamb. (Revelation 7:9, 10) These are they which came out of great tribulation and have washed their robes and made them white in the blood of the Lamb. They shall hunger no more, for the Lamb shall feed them, and lead them unto living fountains and God shall wipe away all tears from their eyes. (Revelation 7:14, 16, 17)

SEVEN TRUMPET ANGELS Pages 26-29

And seven angels stood before God, and unto them were given seven trumpets, and they prepared themselves to sound. (Revelation 8:2, 6) Hear, all ye people and hearken, O earth, all that therein is, for behold the Lord cometh forth out of his holy place and he will come down and tread upon the high places. The mountains shall be molten under his feet, and the valleys cleft as wax before the fire. (Micah 1:2-4) So that the fishes of the sea, and fowls of the heaven, and the beasts of the field, and all that creepeth upon the earth and all the men shall shake at his presence. (Ezekiel 38:20) And the first angel sounded and there followed hail and fire mingled with blood, and they were cast upon the earth, and a third of the trees and all the green grass was burned. And the second angel sounded, and as it were a great mountain burning with fire was cast into the sea, and a third part of the sea became blood, and a third of the creatures died and a third of the ships were destroyed. And the third angel sounded, and there fell a great star upon the third of the rivers and springs of waters, and many men died of the waters, because they were made bitter. And the fourth angel sounded, and a third of the sun, and a third of the moon, and a third of the stars were darkened. (Revelation 8:7-12) And the fifth angel sounded, and there fell a star from heaven, and unto him was given the keys to the bottomless pit. When he opened the pit there came forth locusts upon the earth with the power of scorpion. And they were commanded to torment those men who have not the seal of the living God. (Revelation 9:1-4) And the sixth angel sounded, and a voice from the altar said, Release the four angels who are bound at the great river Euphrates, the angels prepared for the hour and the day and the month and the year to slay a third of mankind. (Revelation 9:13-15) But in the days of the voice of the seventh angel, when he shall begin to sound, the mystery of God should be complete, as declared to his servants the prophets. (Revelation 10:7)

ANGEL STANDING UPON THE LAND AND SEA Pages 30-31

The Lord hath prepared his throne in the heavens, and his kingdom ruleth over all. (Psalm 103:19) Hell is naked before him, and destruction hath no covering. He stretcheth out the north over the empty place, and hangeth the earth upon nothing. (Job 26:6-7) He hath compassed the waters with bounds until the day and night come to an end. The pillars of heaven tremble and are astonished at his reproof. (Job 26:10-11) As for man, his days are as grass, as a flower of the field so he flourisheth. For the wind passeth over it and it is gone, and the place thereof shall know it no more. But the mercy of the Lord is from everlasting to everlasting upon them that fear him, and his righteousness unto children's children. (Psalm 103:15-17) And another mighty angel came down from heaven, (Revelation 10:1) and he set his right foot upon the sea, and his

left foot on the earth, (Revelation 10:2) and lifted up his hand to heaven, and sware by him that liveth for ever and ever that there should be time no longer. (Revelation 10:5-6)

TWO WITNESSES   Pages 32-33

And behold, I will give power unto my two witnesses, and they will prophesy a thousand and two hundred and three score days, clothed in sackcloth. And these are the two olive trees and the two candlesticks standing before the God of the earth. (Revelation 11:3, 4) And when they shall have finished their testimony, the beast that ascendeth out of the bottomless pit shall make war with them, and overcome and kill them. (Revelation 11:7) And after three days and an half the Spirit of life from God entered them, and they stood upon their feet. And they ascended up into heaven in a cloud, and their enemies beheld them. (Revelation 11:11, 12). And the seventh angel sounded, and there were great voices in heaven saying, The kingdoms of this world are become the kingdoms of our Lord and of his Christ, and he shall reign for ever and ever. (Revelation 11:15) We give thee thanks O Lord God Almighty who is, and was, and who is to come, because thou hast taken to thee thy great power, and hast reigned. And the nations were angry, and thy wrath is come, and the time of the dead that they should be judged, and that thou shouldest give reward unto thy servants the prophets, and to the saints, and to them that fear thee both great and small, and shouldest destroy them which destroy the earth. (Revelation 11:17-18)

WOMAN IN TRAVAIL   Page 34-35

And there appeared a great wonder in the heaven, a woman clothed with the sun and the moon under her feet and upon her head a crown of twelve stars, and she being with child cried, travailing in birth and was pained to be delivered. And there appeared another wonder in the heaven behold a red dragon, and the dragon stood before the woman for to devour her child as soon as it was born. And she brought forth a man child who was to rule all nations with a rod of iron, and the child was caught up unto God and to his throne. (Revelation 12:1-5) Now why dost thou cry aloud! is there no king in thee! is thy counsellor perished! For the pangs have taken thee as a woman in travail. (Micah 4:9) Shall I bring to the birth and not cause to bring forth! saith the Lord: shall I cause to bring forth and shut up the womb! saith thy God. Rejoice ye with Jerusalem, and be glad with her, all ye that love her. (Isaiah 66:9, 10)

MICHAEL AND SATAN   Pages 36-37

And there was war in heaven, Michael and his angels fought against the dragon and the dragon fought and his angels, and prevailed not, neither was their place found any more in heaven. And the great dragon was cast out, that old serpent called the Devil and Satan, which deceiveth the whole world, was cast out into the earth. (Revelation 12:7-9) How art thou fallen from heaven, O Lucifer, son of the morning! how art thou cut down to the ground, which didst weaken the nations. For thou hast said in thine heart, I will ascend into heaven, I will exalt my throne above the stars of God, I will sit upon the mount of the congregation, in the sides of the north, I will ascend above the heights of the clouds, I will be like the most High. (Isaiah 14:12-14) O covering cherub, from the midst of the stones of fire, thine heart was lifted up because of thy beauty, thou hast corrupted thy wisdom by reason of thy brightness, and I will cast thee to the ground. (Ezekiel 28:16, 17) Woe to the inhabiters of the earth, for the devil is come down unto you. (Revelation 12:12)

SEVEN VIALS   Pages 38-39

And an angel did fly in the midst of heaven, having the everlasting gospel, saying with a loud voice, Fear God, and give glory to him, for the hour of his judgement is come, and worship him that made heaven, and earth, and the sea, and the fountains of waters. (Revelation 14:6, 7) And there appeared another sign in heaven, great and marvelous, seven angels having the seven last plagues. (Revelation 15:1) The temple in heaven was opened and the seven angels came out of the temple. (Revelation 15:5-6) And them that had gotten the victory did sing the song of Moses, and the song of the Lamb, saying, Great and marvelous are thy works, Lord God Almighty, just and true are thy ways, thou King of saints. Who shall not fear thee and glorify thy name, for thou only art holy, for all nations shall come and worship before thee, for thy judgements are made manifest. (Revelation 15:2-4) And a great voice out of the temple said, Go your ways and pour out the vials of the wrath of God upon the earth. (Revelation 16:1)

ARMAGEDDON   Pages 40-41

And the water of the great river Euphrates was dried up, that the way of the kings of the east might be prepared. And the kings of the whole world were gathered together to the battle of that great day of the Almighty. And they were gathered into a place called Armageddon. (Revelation 16:12, 14, 16) Proclaim ye this among the Gentiles, Prepare war, wake up the

mighty men, let all the men of war draw near. Beat your plowshares into swords, and your scythes into spears. Let the weak say I am strong. (Joel 3:9-10) Assemble yourselves and come, all ye heathen, and gather yourselves together round about, thither cause thy mighty ones to come down, O Lord. Let the heathen be wakened, and come up to the valley, for there will I sit to judge all the heathen round about. Put ye in the sickle, for the harvest is ripe, come, get you down, for the press is full, the fats overflow for their wickedness is great. Multitudes, multitudes in the valley of decision, for the day of the Lord is near in the valley of decision. The Lord shall roar out of Zion, and utter his voice in Jerusalem, and the heavens and the earth shall shake. (Joel 3:11-14, 16) In the hand of the Lord there is a cup, and he poureth out the wine that is red and full. Surely the wicked of the earth must drain the cup and drink it down to the dregs. (Psalm 75:8) And there came a great voice out of heavensaying, It is done, It is done. (Revelation 16:17)

HARLOT OF BABYLON   Pages 42-43

Come hither, and see the judgment of the great harlot that sitteth upon many waters, with whom the kings of the earth have committed fornication, and the inhabitants of the earth have been made drunk with the wine of her fornication. Come hither and see a woman arrayed in scarlet and purple, having a golden cup in her hand, full of abominations and filth of fornication. Come hither and see, she sits upon a scarlet coloured beast full of names of blasphemy, having seven heads and ten horns, a woman drunken with the blood of the martyrs of Jesus. And upon her forehead was written a name of mystery, Babylon the Great, the Mother of Harlots and Abominations of the Earth. (Revelation 17:1-6) Come down and sit in the dust, O virgin daughter of Babylon, sit on the ground with no throne. For thou, O daughter of Chaldeans, art no more tender and delicate. Uncover thy locks, make bare the leg, uncover the thigh, pass over the rivers. (Isaiah 47:1, 2) Show the nations thy nakedness, and the kingdoms thy shame. (Nahum 3:5) Stand with thine enchantments, thy multitude of sorceries. Let now the astrologers and stargazers save thee from the things which shall come upon thee. (Isaiah 47:12,13) Alas, great city, what city is like this great city, wherein were made rich all they that had ships in the sea? (Revelation 18:18, 19) Merchants of the earth, weep and mourn over her. (Revelation 18:11) Come out of her, oh my people, that ye be not partakers of her sins. (Revelation 18:4) Rejoice over her, thou heaven, rejoice ye holy apostles and prophets rejoice. (Revelation 18:20) Babylon is fallen, is fallen, thrown down with violence and become the habitation of dragons. (Revelation 18:2)

FAITHFUL AND TRUE   Pages 44-47

And the heaven opened and behold a white horse, and he that sat upon him was called Faithful and True, and in his righteousness he doth judge and make war. His eyes were as a flame of fire and on his head were many crowns, and he had a name written, that no man knew, but he himself. And he was clothed with a vesture dipped in blood and his name is called the Word of God. And the armies which were in heaven followed him upon white horses clothed in fine linen, white and clean, and out of his mouth goeth a sharp sword that with it he should smite the nations and he shall rule them with a rod of iron and he treadeth the winepress of the fierceness and wrath of God Almighty. And he hath on his vesture and on his thigh a name written King of Kings and Lord of Lords. (Revelation 19:11-16) Who is this that cometh from Edom, with dyed garments from Bozrah, this that is glorious in his apparel, travelling in the greatness of his strength? I that speak in righteousness, mighty to save. Wherefore art thou red in thine apparel and thy garments like him that treadeth in the winefat? I have trodden the winepress alone, and of the people there was none with me, for I will trample them in my fury and their blood shall be sprinkled upon my garments and I will stain all my raiment. For the day of vengence is in mine heart and the year of my redeemed is come. (Isaiah 63:1-4) Behold, thou art fairer than the children of men, grace is poured into thy lips, therefore God hath blessed thee for ever. Gird thy sword upon thy thigh, O most mighty, with thy glory and thy majesty. And in thy majesty ride prosperously because of truth and meekness, and thy right hand shall teach thee terrible things. Thy throne, O God, is for ever and ever, the sceptre of thy kingdom is a right sceptre. (Psalm 45:2, 3, 4, 6) O praise ye the Lord. Praise ye the Lord from the heavens, praise him in the heights. Praise ye him, all his angels, praise ye him, all his hosts. Praise ye him, sun and moon, praise him, all ye stars of light, praise him, ye heavens of heavens, and ye waters that be above the heavens. Let them praise the name of the Lord for he commanded and they were created. He hath also stablished them for ever and ever, he hath made a decree which shall not pass. Praise the Lord from the earth, ye dragons and all deeps, fire and hail, snow and vapours, stormy wind fulfilling his word, mountains and all hills, fruitful trees and all cedars, beasts and all cattle, creeping things and flying fowl, kings of the earth and all people, princes and all judges of the earth, both young men and maidens, old men and children, let them praise the name of the Lord for his name alone is excellent, his glory above the earth and heaven. (Psalm 148:1-13)

THE HOLY CITY   Pages 48-50

And behold a great white throne and him that sat upon it, from whose face the earth and the heaven are fled away, and the dead, small and great, stand before God, and the books were opened, and the dead were judged out of those things which were written in the books accord-

ing to their works. (Revelation 20:11, 12) And behold the holy city, new Jerusalem, coming down from God out of heaven, prepared as a bride adorned for her husband, having the glory of God, and her light was like unto a stone most precious, even like jasper, clear as crystal. And the city had no need of the sun, neither of the moon, to shine in it, for the glory of God did lighten it, and the Lamb is the light thereof. (Revelation 21:2, 11, 23) Awake, awake, put on thy strength, O Zion, put on thy beautiful garments, O Jerusalem, the holy city. (Isaiah 52:1) Blessed be the Lord, who layeth the beams of his chambers in the waters, who maketh the clouds his chariot, who walketh upon the wings of the wind. (Psalm 104:3) And a great voice out of heaven was heard, saying, Behold, the tabernacle of God is with men, and he will dwell with them, and they shall be his people. And God shall wipe away all tears from their eyes, and there shall be no more death, neither sorrow, nor crying, neither shall there be any more pain, for the former things are passed away. (Revelation 21:3-4) And there shall be no more curse. (Revelation 22:3) O clap your hands, all ye people, shout unto God with a voice of triumph. (Psalm 47:1) Behold I make all things new. It is done. I am Alpha and Omega, the beginning and the end. I will give unto him that is athirst of the fountain of the water of life freely. (Revelation 21:5, 6) I am he that liveth, and was dead, and behold I am alive forevermore, Amen, and have the keys of hell and death. (Revelation 1:18) Behold, I create new heavens and a new earth, and the former shall not be remembered, nor brought to mind. But be ye glad and rejoice forever in that which I create, for behold, I create Jerusalem a rejoicing, and her people a joy. (Isaiah 65:17, 18) Praise ye the Lord. Praise God in his sanctuary, praise him in the firmament of his power. Praise him for his mighty acts, praise him according to his excellent greatness. (Psalm 150:1-2) Let everything that hath breath praise the Lord. Praise ye the Lord. (Psalm 150:6) Even so, come Lord Jesus. The grace of our Lord Jesus Christ be with you all. Amen and Amen. (Revelation 22:20, 21)

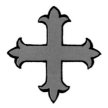

The paintings in this book were begun in 1971 and completed in 1975. They were executed in mixed media on a gessoed panel with various binding vehicles, including distemper, egg tempera, oil, and gold leaf.

The calligraphy hand is a variation, devised by Mary Breeden, of Uncial script, and was written in hand-ground ink. The borders around the calligraphy were painted in hand-mixed egg tempera and 22-karat gold leaf.

The front and back matter of the book was set in a typeface called Post Antiqua. The book was printed on 106-pound New Age Matte paper. The separations and the printing were done by the Toppan Printing Company in Tokyo, Japan.